From Egg to Adult
The Life Cycle of Insects

Richard and Louise
Spilsbury

Heinemann Library
Chicago, Illinois

Customer Service 888-454-2279
Visit our website at www.heinemannlibrary.com

Editing, Design, Photo Research, and Production by Heinemann Library
Illustrations by David Woodroffe
Originated by Dot Gradations Ltd
Printed in China by Wing King Tong

07 06 05 04 03
10 9 8 7 6 5 4 3 2 1

Library of Congress Cataloging-in-Publication Data
Spilsbury, Louise.
   The life cycle of insects / Louise & Richard Spilsbury.
     p. cm. -- (From egg to adult)
   Summary: Discusses how insects differ from other animals,
 their habitat, what they eat, how they are born and develop, how
 they reproduce, and their typical life expectancy.
   Includes bibliographical references (p.   ).
   ISBN 1-4034-0786-X (HC) 1-4034-3406-9 (PB)
   1. Insects--Life cycles--Juvenile literature.   [1. Insects.]

   I. Spilsbury, Richard, 1963-   . II. Title. III. Series.
   QL467.2.S73 2003
   595.7--dc21

                              2002011709

Acknowledgments
The Publishers would like to thank the following for permission to reproduce photographs:
p. 4 NHPA/A.N.T.; p. 5 Ardea/I. R. Beames; p. 6 NHPA/G. I. Bernard; p. 7 Oxford Scientific Films; pp. 8, 21 Ardea/Steve Hopkin; p. 10 Ardea/John Mason; p. 11 Bruce Coelman/Joe McDonald; p. 12 Ardea/Elizabeth S. Burgess; p. 13 Ardea/Pascal Goetgheluck; p. 14 Ardea/Pat Morris; p. 15 Oxford Scientific Films/Davis Shale/SAL; p. 16 Oxford Scientific Films/Roland Mayr; p. 17 FLPA/G. E. Hyde; p. 18 (left) FLPA/Jeremy Early; pp. 18 (right), 20 NHPA/Stephen Dalton; p. 19 FLPA/B. Borrell; p. 22 NHPA/G. J. Cambridge; p. 24 (top) FLPA/T. S. Zylva; p. 24 (bottom) FLPA/J. van Arkel/Foto Natura; p. 25 Oxford Scientific Films/Richard Davies; p. 26 FLPA/Minden Pictures.

Cover photograph of the emperor dragonfly, reproduced with permission of FLPA.

The insect at the top of each page is a green shield beetle.

Every effort has been made to contact copyright holders of any material reproduced in this book. Any omissions will be rectified in subsequent printings if notice is given to the Publishers.

Some words are shown in bold, **like this.** You can find out what they mean by looking in the glossary.

Contents

Look but don't touch: Many insects are easily hurt and may sting or bite. If you see one in the wild, do not get too close to it. Look at it, but do not try to touch it!

What Is an Insect?

Insects are small animals such as flies and ants. They are **invertebrates,** which means they do not have a backbone to protect and support their bodies. Instead, insects have tough skin called an **exoskeleton** that covers and supports their soft bodies.

A world of insects

There are more than 900,000 known **species** of insects on Earth. All plants and all other animals make up only 550,000 species put together!

Body matters

An adult insect's body is made up of three main sections—a head, thorax, and abdomen. Its head has eyes and **antennae,** or feelers, for sensing the world around it and a mouth for eating. Its thorax has six legs and may also have two pairs of wings. Its abdomen contains parts for breathing, for **digesting** food, and for **reproducing.**

Like other adult insects, this German wasp has six legs and three body sections.

head

thorax

abdomen

How Are Insects Born?

When baby insects are born, they hatch from eggs. Insect eggs come in a variety of shapes, colors, and patterns, but most are oval or round and pale or cream colored. The eggs of the smallest insects can be seen only under a microscope. Bigger insects usually lay larger eggs. The longest stick insects lay eggs measuring nearly a half inch (1 centimeter) long.

These butterfly eggs are just a few millimeters across. They have a patterned surface.

Inside insect eggs

Insect eggs contain a central **yolk.** Part of the yolk develops into an **embryo.** The other part of the yolk is a supply of food that provides **energy** for the embryo to grow bigger and stronger.

An insect egg has a thin outer layer called a chorion, which can be smooth or rough. The chorion protects the embryo inside the egg and helps keep it from drying out. It is not as tough as the shell on bird or reptile eggs, though.

Egg numbers

Female adult insects lay eggs. Different female insects lay different numbers of eggs during their lifetime. The number varies for many reasons, such as how much food the female has eaten and what **species** she belongs to. For example, a female that has not found much food to eat does not have enough energy to make many eggs. Most females lay 100 to 200 eggs. Some, such as scarab beetles, lay around 10 during their life, but others lay thousands. Termite **queens** can produce 10,000 to 30,000 eggs every day!

Arranging eggs

Some insects, such as longhorn beetles, lay eggs one by one. Other insects, such as cockroaches, lay up to 50 eggs at a time, in a case. This case protects them like an egg carton. Mayflies lay eggs on the surface of lakes as they fly over them.

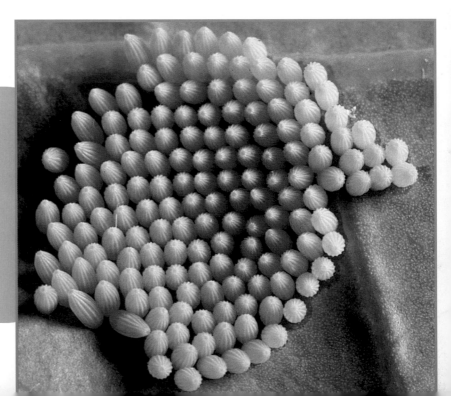

Many butterflies, such as cabbage white butterflies, lay their eggs in big clusters in one place.

Breaking out

Insect embryos grow inside their eggs until they are ready to hatch. Some insect eggs hatch soon after they are laid. Some mosquito eggs hatch within a few hours. Other eggs take much longer. Some stick insect eggs have tough shells to protect the embryos inside for up to two years as they slowly develop.

Odd ones out?

Some baby insects seem to come straight out of their mothers, not from eggs. A female hissing cockroach's eggs actually hatch as they are being laid, so the nymphs look as if they are being born live.

The baby insects that hatch from eggs are called **larvae** or **nymphs,** depending on the type of insect. They wriggle and break open their egg, often eating the chorion shell as they go. This provides a first meal.

These butterfly larvae hatch together because their eggs were laid in the same place at the same time.

7

Who Takes Care of Baby Insects?

When a young insect comes out of its egg, it is tiny and alone. Most young insects never even see their parents, and they never get any help or protection from them.

Once insect parents have produced eggs, their task—to **reproduce**—is complete. A few, such as mayflies, die, worn out and unable to eat. Others, such as houseflies, leave their eggs and fly off to reproduce elsewhere.

Different looks

Most young insects look different from their parents. Some, such as butterfly or moth larvae, look totally different from their parents. Others, such as grasshopper or springtail **nymphs,** look more like tiny versions of their parents.

Caring parents

Some insect females, such as earwigs, take care of their young, but very few males do. Both male and female burying beetles care for their **larvae,** providing food and defending them from **predators**—animals that want to eat them.

Female earwigs have jawlike pincers on their abdomen. They use this weapon to defend their larvae from danger until the larvae grow pincers of their own.

Dangerous start

Larvae and nymphs are usually only a few millimeters long when they hatch. They have no wings, and their legs are often short so they cannot move very fast. This means it is easy for predators such as birds, frogs, and fish to catch them.

Newly hatched young insects have different ways of keeping out of sight of predators. Many are **camouflaged**—they are the same color or pattern as the places where they live. For example, cabbage white butterfly larvae are green to match the leaves their parents laid their eggs on. Others keep out of sight in other ways. Mosquito larvae hatch underwater and float at the surface, breathing air through tubes like snorkels. They dive to darker water below when danger approaches.

A female monarch butterfly lays about 700 eggs in her life. Of these, only about 100 will survive to become adults. For most insects, even fewer young will make it from egg to adult.

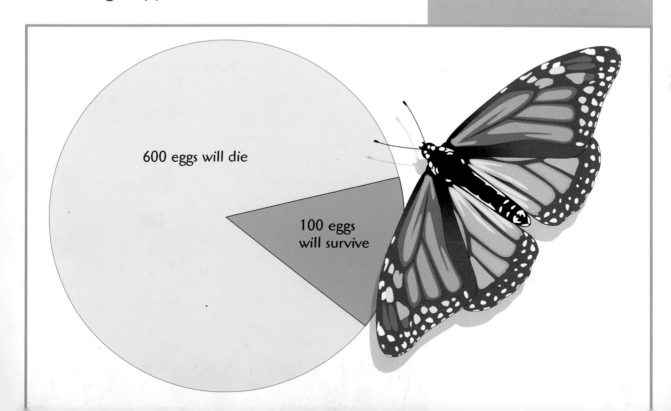

600 eggs will die

100 eggs will survive

Life in a nest

Some types of insects almost always live in big groups in one nest. Bees, wasps, ants, and termites are called **social insects.** Hundreds of thousands may live together in a nest that they build. Not all social insects in one nest look the same or do the same things. They all work together to take care of the group's young.

Baby social insects, such as these bee larvae, are fed and protected by many bee adults in the safety of their nest.

In each social insect nest, one **queen** lays all the eggs. Most of her eggs hatch into females that cannot **reproduce.** Groups of these females—called workers— take care of the queen's eggs or gather food for the **larvae,** queen, and other workers. Some workers are called soldiers. Ant soldiers have large jaws to defend the nest and the ants inside from **predators.** At certain times of year, a few of the queen's eggs hatch into winged insects whose job is to reproduce. Winged males—often called drones—fly from the nest chasing new queens. After they have mated, the queens start new nests, but the winged males die.

How Do Baby Insects Grow Bigger?

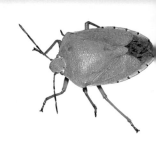

Insects grow differently from people. As we gradually get bigger, our skeletons inside get bigger too. An insect's rigid **exoskeleton** does not grow. So how do insects' insides grow bigger?

When an exoskeleton becomes too tight around the growing body inside, it splits, and the insect peels it off. This is called **molting.** A new soft exoskeleton waits under the old one. The insect puffs up its body with air and the new, bigger exoskeleton hardens. Most insect larvae molt about 5 times before they become adults, but some, such as mayflies, may molt 45 times.

Ways of growing

Different insect **species** grow up in different ways. Most young insects grow wings as they change into adults, but there are other changes as well, called **metamorphosis.** A few species, such as silverfish, change very little as they grow and never have wings.

Just as children outgrow their clothes, insects, such as this cicada, outgrow their exoskeletons.

Types of changes

Some young insects, such as grasshoppers, hatch as **nymphs** that look sort of like the adults but with no wings. After each **molt,** they gradually grow wings. After the final molt, they become adults that can fly and **reproduce.** This is called incomplete **metamorphosis.**

Out of the water

Damselfly nymphs live in water and breathe using gills (body parts used for breathing under water). Before the final molt, they crawl out of the water and metamorphose into winged, air-breathing adults.

Complete metamorphosis happens in most insects, including moths, beetles, and flies. They have four separate life stages—egg, larva, **pupa,** and adult. **Larvae**—often called caterpillars, grubs, or maggots—have very tiny legs, or no legs at all. When a larva is fully grown, its exoskeleton splits to reveal a pupa. A pupa is like a sealed case. The larva changes into an adult insect inside this case. When the adult breaks out, it waits for its wings to unfold and for its **exoskeleton** to harden.

This butterfly pupa has changed into an adult, which breaks out after several weeks.

Speed of growth

Insect larvae grow very quickly when they can find enough food to eat. A monarch butterfly caterpillar may increase its weight by 2,000 times in two weeks. Big larvae usually metamorphose into bigger adults. But the size of an adult also depends on the size and fitness of its parents.

This rhinoceros beetle grub goes into a deep sleep called hibernation to survive cold times.

The speed of metamorphosis varies with how warm it is. Insects that live in warm places may metamorphose in a few weeks. Metamorphosis may take longer for insects that live in places with cold winters. Rove beetles may spend winter as larvae, often protected from the cold by digging underground. In spring, when it is warmer, they leave their shelter to complete their metamorphosis. Larger larvae change into pupae during winter and break out as adults in spring.

How Do Insects Get Food?

The mouths of insects are specially shaped depending on the type of food they eat.

*Adult butterflies have a thin coiled **proboscis** that they straighten out like a party blower to drink flower nectar.*

Some insects are chewers. Like all insects, their mouths have no teeth inside. Instead they are shaped like jagged scissors that move from side to side. Some chewing insects, such as termites, eat plants, but others, such as praying mantises, are carnivores—they chew and eat other animals.

Other insects are suckers. Their mouths are shaped like straws. Shield bugs stick their mouths into plant stems to drink sweet **sap.** Mosquitoes stick their sharp mouths into animals to drink blood. They make a special chemical in their **saliva** that keeps the blood from **clotting** so they can drink more.

Soakers

Some flies have special mouths with a spongelike lower lip. They vomit saliva and stomach juices onto food to dissolve it and then soak up the liquid.

Types of food

Insects eat a wide range of food, from plants to animals, living or dead. Some feed on anything, but others can feed only on a certain food. For example, the Darwin's hawk-moth of Madagascar has a proboscis about 12 inches (30 centimeters) long that it uses to feed on **nectar** only from certain orchids with long flowers. Many young insects eat different food than adults do. For example, lacewing adults drink sap, but their **larvae** eat aphids and leafhoppers.

Many insects are scavengers. They eat dead animals that they find. Burying beetles dig under dead animals to bury them and then eat the flesh. Some insects eat dung, the solid waste of animals. Dung beetles roll balls of dung into **burrows.** Adults and larvae then eat up the dung. By doing so, they help keep the Earth clean.

Swarms of locusts eat any type of plant they come across.

Getting food

Insects have various tricks to make sure they catch food. Some, such as ants, poison their **prey** to knock them out. Others make special traps. Ant-lion **larvae** make pits in sand $1^1/_4$ inches (3 centimeters) across and hide at the bottom. Ants that walk by fall down the sloping sides and are trapped in the ant-lion's massive jaws. Some caddisfly larvae spin silk nets underwater to catch swimming prey. A few species of ants are farmers—they take care of herds of aphids because the aphids make a sweet fluid that the ants like to eat.

Using senses

Insects use various senses for finding food. Most insects have eyes made up of thousands of separate **lenses** that can sense movement all around them. Blood-sucking midges find people to attack by using their **antennae** to "smell" sweat. Butterflies "taste" plants with their feet!

A praying mantis can twist its head almost completely around on its neck to see prey.

How Do Insects Grow Up Safely?

Insects are a favorite food of many animals, including anteaters, bats, frogs, spiders, and shrews, as well as other insects and plants such as Venus's fly-traps. Insects use different ways of avoiding being eaten so they can grow up safely.

The right appearance

Many insects avoid **predators** by how they look. Some are **camouflaged.** This means that they have patterns, shapes, and colors that make them look like their surroundings. Stick insects are long and thin and look like twigs. Flower mantids have bright colors and a frilly abdomen to look like petals. Other insects even look like bird droppings or thorns.

Some insects use color differently. They are brightly colored so they will be noticed. The bold red and black patterns on burnet moths and ladybird beetles warn predators that they taste bad.

The elephant hawk-moth caterpillar sucks in air and puffs up the skin behind its head to look like a snake if danger approaches.

Weapons

Many insects are equipped with weapons to fight back if predators come near. Female wasps, bees, and some ants have stingers. These are sharp, arrow-shaped tubes at the end of their abdomen. Stingers are connected to **sacs** of **venom** (poisonous chemicals). They plunge the sting into other animals and inject their venom.

Other insects have different ways of delivering a nasty surprise. Wood ants spray **acid,** and bombardier beetles spray an irritating gas. Saddleback and puss caterpillars are covered with thin, hair-like spines that break off and stick in the skin of predators. Monarch caterpillars eat poisonous milkweed leaves. Its poison does not affect the caterpillars, but it makes their bodies taste bad to **predators.**

Cheats

Yellow and black bands on the abdomen of a wasp or bee warn predators about its harmful sting. Harmless hoverflies and moths trick predators because they have similar stripes. They look like wasps but do not have stingers.

A beefly (left) has no stinger, but it looks kind of like a bumblebee (right), which does!

Getting away

Most insects see predators coming, but they may also sense danger using tiny hairs on their bodies. An approaching predator causes tiny air movements. Insects can feel these movements through their hairs. They react rapidly and escape. Houseflies fly away, beating their wings 20,000 times a minute. Grasshoppers jump away, using strong, long back legs. Fleas can jump distances 200 times longer than their body length using **energy** stored in special muscles.

Out of sight

Many insects are small enough to be able to hide pretty well. Some, such as moths and bedbugs, come out only at night when they cannot be seen by most predators. Other insects take cover in special places to avoid predators. For example, fleas hide among **mammal** hair instead of on open skin. Termites and other **social insects** build tough nests.

*Caddisfly **larvae** make tubes covered with rocks or sticks in which to hide from predators.*

When Is an Insect Grown Up?

An insect is grown up after it has completed its **metamorphosis.** It has now stopped growing and **molting,** and it is ready to start **breeding.** Once it is grown up, it does not need to eat as much or as often as when it was young. It no longer needs **energy** to grow.

The entire life cycle of most insects—from egg to adult—usually lasts between two weeks and eight months. It may be much quicker—some aphids take less than a week—but can be much longer. Some beetles that live in wood inside trees may live for 40 years before they complete metamorphosis. Most insects spend a much longer time as eggs, **larvae,** and pupae than they do as adults.

These elm bark beetle larvae are feeding on the wood in which they live.

How Do Insects Have Babies?

When they are grown up, insects are ready to **reproduce.**
A female can usually only reproduce if she can find a male to
fertilize her eggs with his **sperm.**

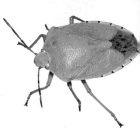

Keeping other males away

Male insects often compete
to get a female to mate with.
Some males take over an
area—called a territory—as
their own and try to keep
other males out. For example,
dragonflies defend stretches
of riverbank that have water
plants. Males often fight over
these territories because they
are good places for females
to lay eggs.

*This male dung fly
defends a cow pie—his
territory—from other
males because females
like to lay their eggs
there.*

The big flight

Male midges fly together in big
swarms to mate. This is called a
nuptial flight. Females are more
likely to find males in a swarm
than if they are alone.

Sensing partners

Insects use senses, such as hearing, taste, and sight, to find a mate. Male short-horned grasshoppers make a noise by rubbing their back legs against their wings—kind of like moving a bow across the strings on a violin. Cicadas have two patches of **exoskeleton** on their **abdomen,** which they move quickly back and forth to make a loud call. The biggest, fittest males usually have the loudest call and attract the most females.

Some insects taste the air. Female luna moths produce a special chemical that attracts males. Males have large, feathery **antennae** that can sense tiny amounts of her chemical up to 5 miles (8 kilometers) away.

antennae

The luna moth is furry to help it keep warm at night, when it is active.

Amazing light

Some insects put on light displays. Male fireflies and female glowworms have special chemicals in their abdomens that make bright lights. Each species flashes its lights on and off at night in a slightly different pattern to make sure they attract the right partner.

Courtship

When a male has found a female, he often moves or behaves in particular ways to make sure mating actually happens. This is called courtship. Male mosquitoes and mayflies dance in flight. Some mantids stroke each other's antennae and move slowly next to each other until the female is ready to mate. This can be risky for males, who may be eaten by the females if they do not make the right moves. Springtail males make a circle of **sperm** packets—the female then chooses one to fertilize her eggs.

The right timing

Many insects reproduce in certain seasons, usually when the weather is warm and dry, so their eggs have a better chance of hatching successfully. These times are called **breeding** seasons. Breeding seasons can be short in cold places but long in areas where it is warm all year round. Some insects, such as monarch butterflies, travel long distances to return to the same place to mate each year.

Female insects usually lay eggs where their young can find food easily. The female potter wasp uses her stinger to **paralyze** a caterpillar, puts it into her cone-shaped mud nest, and lays eggs on it. When her **larvae** hatch, they eat the still-living caterpillar.

Many insects hide their eggs for protection. Female crickets have a long spike called an ovipositor at the end of their abdomen. They use it to lay eggs underground. This protects them from getting damaged by frost or being found by **predators.**

ovipositer

How Old Do Insects Get?

An animal's life expectancy is the length of time it can live. Human life expectancy is about 70 years. Most insects hatch, grow up, and die in less than a year. Others live for much shorter lengths of time. Some fruit flies live for only two weeks. There are a few **species** that live for much longer. For example, **queen** termites may live more than 30 years.

Most insects never reach their full life expectancy. They, like other animals, can survive only if they find enough food and water and avoid disease, **parasites,** and **predators.**

Brief adult life

One type of mayfly usually lives for about a year. Almost all this time is spent under water as a **nymph.** After **molting** to become a grown-up, it usually lives for just five minutes. In this brief time, it mates and then dies.

This larva-like queen termite has a massive abdomen full of eggs. She usually lives a long time because she is protected and fed by other termites in the nest.

People and insects

Some insects, such as mosquitoes and fleas, spread diseases among people. They feed on the blood of a sick person or animal and then pass on the disease when they bite another person. Other insects, such as locusts and weevils, destroy crops. Still others, such as warble fly **larvae,** injure or even kill farm animals by eating their flesh. Deathwatch beetles and carpenter ants damage wooden buildings and furniture.

Since insects are seen as a pest, people have become the biggest threat to insect populations. To kill problem insects, people have developed powerful chemicals called insecticides or pesticides. Unfortunately, such chemicals damage natural **habitats** and other living things.

*Many harmless insects are killed when their habitats are destroyed or changed by people. When people cut down **tropical rain forests,** they may be destroying thousands of unknown insect species. This karyatid was discovered in the tropical rain forest in Costa Rica.*

Life cycles

The age that an insect reaches is not important to whether its **species** lives on. The important thing is how many young it produces that live to adulthood and have young of their own. This is the cycle of life—from egg to adult to egg. The young are born, grow, and produce young themselves before they die. This cycle of life must be completed for each individual insect to help its species live on.

Insect math challenge

Imagine that a male and female housefly mated and laid a batch of 100 eggs. Then imagine that each of those eggs developed into adults that each laid 100 eggs. If this went on for four months, that single pair of flies could produce billions of **descendants!**

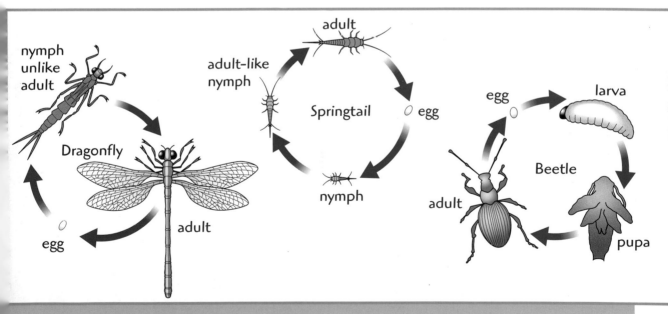

nymph unlike adult

Dragonfly

adult

egg

adult-like nymph

Springtail

egg

nymph

adult

egg

larva

Beetle

pupa

adult

Most insects, such as beetles, change from egg to larva to **pupa** to adult. This is called complete **metamorphosis.** Other insects change from egg to **nymph** to adult, which is called incomplete metamorphosis. In some insects, such as springtails, the nymphs are similar to adults. But in others, such as dragonflies, they are very different.

Fact File

What is . . .

- **the fastest metamorphosis from egg to adult?**
Some aphids take five days, and some mosquitoes seven days.

- **the slowest metamorphosis from egg to adult?**
Some wood-boring beetles may take more than 40 years to become an adult.

- **the smallest egg?**
The fairy fly, a kind of wasp, lays the smallest egg. It is only about as wide as a hair.

- **the largest number of molts in a lifetime?**
Silverfish change their **exoskeletons** 50 times.

- **the smallest number of young produced in one lifetime?**
Louse flies produce an average of four babies in their lifetime.

- **the largest number of young produced in one lifetime?**
An African driver ant queen may lay up to 3 million eggs in a month!

- **the largest wingspan?**
The atlas moth measures 12 inches (30 centimeters) from wing tip to wing tip.

- **the heaviest insect?**
Adult goliath beetles can weigh up to 3.5 ounces (100 grams).

- **the longest and smallest insects?**
Adult walkingstick insects can reach 20 inches (50 centimeters) long. Eight adult parasitic wasps end to end would measure about $^4/_{100}$ inch (1 millimeter).

Insect Classification

Insects that look similar or have similar life cycles are generally grouped together. Such grouping—called classification—helps make sense of the huge numbers of different insects on Earth. It also helps us to figure out how they might be related to one another. Of the 30 or so main groups, called orders, the most familiar include beetles, butterflies, moths, and flies.

Unknown numbers

No one knows exactly how many **species** of insects live on Earth. Some scientists think there may be about 30 million, but others think there are about 6 million. More species are discovered every year. You might need only a few hours in a **tropical rain forest** to find an insect unknown to science.

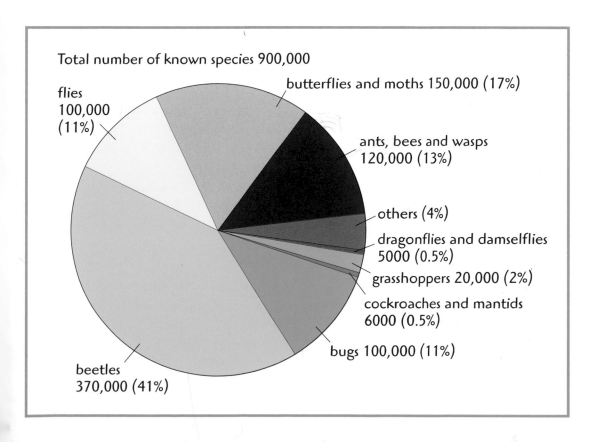

Total number of known species 900,000

butterflies and moths 150,000 (17%)

flies 100,000 (11%)

ants, bees and wasps 120,000 (13%)

others (4%)

dragonflies and damselflies 5000 (0.5%)

grasshoppers 20,000 (2%)

cockroaches and mantids 6000 (0.5%)

bugs 100,000 (11%)

beetles 370,000 (41%)

Glossary

acid liquid that burns skin

antennae pair of feelers on an insect's head used to feel and taste

breed have babies

burrows underground homes of animals

camouflage color or pattern that helps an animal blend in with its surroundings

clotting when blood gets thick and hard to stop a wound from bleeding

descendant Every living thing is a descendant of its parents and grandparents.

digesting breaking down food in the body so it can be used for energy

embryo insect growing inside an egg

energy power of living things to do all the activities that they need to do to live and grow

exoskeleton hard skin that forms a skeleton on the outside of insects and certain other animals

fertilize to cause an egg and sperm to join, which begins the development of an embryo

habitat place where a plant or animal lives.

invertebrate animal without a backbone

larvae young animals that look very different from their parents

lens part of the eye that makes sight clearer

mammal warm-blooded animal with a backbone that feeds its young on mother's milk

metamorphosis change of shape during an animal's life cycle

molt to regularly peel off and replace the skin. Insects and other animals molt.

nectar sweet liquid made in flowers to attract insects

nymph stage in metamorphosis of some insects between egg and adult

paralyze to make something unable to move

parasite living thing that lives on or in another living thing. A parasite often hurts the thing it lives on or in.

predator animal that hunts or catches other animals to eat them

prey animals that are hunted or caught for food by predators

proboscis tubelike organ used for feeding

pupa stage in the metamorphosis of insects between larva and adult

queen largest female in an insect group, which lays all the eggs for the group

reproduce have babies

sacs small baglike parts on an animal

saliva liquid in an animal's mouth that helps it swallow

sap sweet fluid inside plants

social insects insects that live in groups in which each insect has a special job to do

species group of living things that are similar in many ways and can breed to produce healthy babies

sperm a type of cell made by male animals that joins with an egg in fertilization

tropical rain forest thick forest of tall trees that grows in hot, sunny places where it rains almost every day

venom poison made in the bodies of some insects

yolk part of an egg that serves as food for the baby that is growing inside

More Books to Read

Gareth Stevens Publishing Staff. *Insects.* Milwaukee, Wisc.: Gareth Stevens, Inc., 2002.

Hipp, Andrew. *The Life Cycle of a Praying Mantis.* New York: Rosen Publishing Group, Inc., 2002.

Legg, Gerald. *The World of Insect life.* Milwaukee, Wisc.: Gareth Stevens, Inc., 2002.

Meister, Cari. *Dragonflies.* Edina, Minn.: ABDO Publishing Company, 2001.

Milton, Joyce. *Honeybees, Volume 2.* New York: Penguin Putnam Books for Young Readers, 2003.

Mound, Laurence A. *The Insect.* New York: Dorling Kinderley Publishers, Inc., 2001.

National Geographic Society Staff. *Insects.* Washington, D.C.: National Geographic Society, 2001.

Index